This Book Belongs To:

© **Copyright 2024 - All rights reserved.**

You may not reproduce, duplicate or send the contents of this book without direct written permission from the author. You cannot hereby despite any circumstance blame the publisher or hold him or her to legal responsibility for any reparation, compensations, or monetary forfeiture owing to the information included herein, either in a direct or an indirect way.

Legal Notice: This book has copyright protection. You can use the book for personal purposes. You should not sell, use, alter, distribute, quote, take excerpts, or paraphrase in part or whole the material contained in this book without obtaining the permission of the author first.

Disclaimer Notice: You must take note that the information in this document is for casual reading and entertainment purposes only. We have made every attempt to provide accurate, up-to-date, and reliable information. We do not express or imply guarantees of any kind. The persons who read admit that the writer is not occupied in giving legal, financial, medical, or other advice. We put this book content by sourcing various places.

Please consult a licensed professional before you try any techniques shown in this book. By going through this document, the book lover comes to an agreement that under no situation is the author accountable for any forfeiture, direct or indirect, which they may incur because of the use of material contained in this document, including, but not limited to, a errors, omissions, or inaccuracies.

Q: Why don't cats play poker in the jungle?

A: Too many cheetahs!

Q: What do you call a cat that loves to bowl?

A: An alley cat!

Q: How do cats end a fight?

A: They hiss and make up!

Q: What do you call a cat who became a doctor?

A: A first-aid kit!

Q: Why was the cat sitting on the computer?

A: It wanted to keep an eye on the mouse!

Q: What do you call a cat that can put together furniture from Sweden?

A: An assembly purr!

Q: Why do cats always get their way?

A: They are very purr-suasive!

Q: What do you call a cat who loves to eat beans?

A: A gas-tro-nomical kitty!

Q: How do cats maintain law and order?

A: Claw enforcement!

Q: Why was the cat afraid of the tree?

A: Because of its bark!

Q: What do you call a cat that throws all the most expensive parties?

A: The Great Catsby!

Q: What's a cat's favorite magazine?

A: Good Mousekeeping!

Q: Why don't cats like online shopping?

A: They prefer a cat-alog!

Q: What do cats eat for breakfast?

A: Mice Krispies!

Q: How do cats stop crimes?

A: They call in the purr-trol!

Q: What do you call a cat who lives in an igloo?

A: An eskimew!

Q: Why was the cat so good at video games?

A: Because it had nine lives!

Q: What do you call a cat that loves to go jogging?

A: A running purr!

Q: What do you call a cat that does tricks?

A: A magicat!

Q: Why did the cat join the Red Cross?

A: It wanted to be a first-aid purr-amedic!

Q: What do cats wear to bed?

A: Paw-jamas!

Q: What do you call a cat that's a beauty influencer?

A: A glamour puss!

Q: Why do cats always win video games?

A: Because they have nine lives!

Q: What do you call a cat who loves to hike?

A: An adventure paw!

Q: What do you call a cat who's a master at finding things?

A: A purr-sistant detective!

Q: Why don't cats play sports?

A: They get too distracted chasing the ball!

Q: What's a cat's favorite color?

A: Purr-ple!

Q: What do you call a cat who loves to swim?

A: A catfish!

Q: What do you call a well-informed cat?

A: A fact feline!

Q: Why did the cat sit on the computer?

A: It wanted to keep track of the cursor!

Q: What do you call a cat that can pick locks?

A: A cat burglar!

Q: Why was the cat so agitated?

A: It was having a bad fur day!

Q: What do you call a cat that's also a judge?

A: The purr-secutor!

Q: What do you call a cat who loves to cook?

A: A chef purr-son!

Q: Why was the cat sitting with the computer?

A: It was updating its purr-sonal blog!

Q: What do you call a group of cats who start a band?

A: The meow-sicians!

Q: What do you call a cat who's a wizard at math?

A: A fibo-nacho!

Q: How do cats prefer their steak?

A: Purr-fectly rare!

Q: What's a cat's favorite musical instrument?

A: The purr-cussion drums!

Q: What do you call a cat that's also a detective?

A: Sherlock Whiskers!

Q: Why was the cat such a good baseball player?

A: Because it always hit a fur-ball!

Q: What do you call a cat who writes books?

A: A paw-thor!

Q: What do you call a cat who loves to jump into boxes?

A: A box-er!

Q: Why did the cat sit on the computer?

A: To keep an eye on the mouse!

Q: What's a cat's way of keeping law and order?

A: Claw enforcement!

Knock Knock.

Howard

Who's there?

Howard who?

Howard I know you're not a cat if you won't let me in to see!

Knock Knock.

Feline

Who's there?

Feline who?

Feline pretty good about catching that mouse, let me in to brag!

Knock Knock.

Tabby

Who's there?

Tabby who?

Tabby or not tabby, that is the question!

Knock Knock.

Claws

Who's there?

Claws who?

Claws the door, I'm getting cold out here!

Knock Knock.

Whisker

Who's there?

Whisker who?

Whisker me away to a land of endless catnip!

Knock Knock.

Purr

Who's there?

Purr who?

Purr-chance, could you open the door? It's meow-tside!

Knock Knock.

Who's there?

Catnip

Catnip who?

Catnip in the bud, or I'll keep knocking all night!

Knock Knock.

Who's there?

Mews

Mews who?

Mewsic to my ears, open up, I've got tunes to share!

Knock Knock.

Kitty

Who's there?

Kitty who?

Kitty on the roof needs your help, or is it just a purr-ception?

Knock Knock.

Mittens

Who's there?

Mittens who?

Mittens my paws before I freeze out here, let me in!

Knock Knock.

Catsup

Who's there?

Catsup who?

Catsup with me, and I'll tell you a purr-fectly funny story!

Knock Knock.

Sherlock

Who's there?

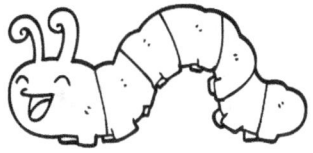

Sherlock who?

Sherlock your doors, there's a cat burglar on the loose!

Knock Knock.

Meow

Who's there?

Meow who?

Me-ow do you do? Just clawed my way over here to hang out!

Knock Knock.

Cattitude

Who's there?

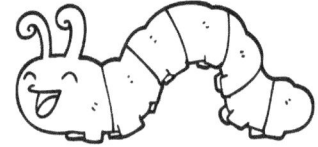

Cattitude who?

Cattitude is everything; now, can I strut into your life like I own the place?

Knock Knock.

Paws

Who's there?

Paws who?

Paws your video game and let me in, I promise I won't bite!

Knock Knock.

Hiss

Who's there?

Hiss who?

Hiss-terical me, just trying to sneak in some puns. Open up!

Knock Knock.

Wifi

Who's there?

Wifi who?

Wifi-ghting this? Let me in so we can stream some cat videos together!

Knock Knock.

Hashtag

Who's there?

Hashtag who?

Hashtag 'CatLife', ready to trend in your living room!

Knock Knock.

Tabby

Who's there?

Tabby who?

Tabby honest, I'm just here for the free Wi-Fi and snacks!

Knock Knock.

Furball

Who's there?

Furball who?

Furball the times we've had, let me in for more purrfect memories!

Knock Knock.

Catnap

Who's there?

Catnap who?

Catnap's over, let me in or I'll start meowing at your window!

Knock Knock.

Who's there?

Whispurr

Whispurr who?

Whispurr me your secrets, I promise I won't tell a soul... except maybe my cat.

Knock Knock.

Meowmix

Who's there?

Meowmix who?

Meowmix it up a bit, let's do something fun tonight!

Knock Knock.

Cat-ch

Who's there?

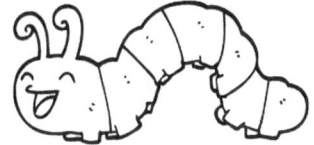

Cat-ch who?

Cat-ch you later if you don't let me in now, I've got nine lives of stories to share!

Knock Knock.

Who's there?

Catapult

Catapult who?

Catapult your spirits, let's pounce on some fun tonight!

Knock Knock.

Who's there?

Clawdia

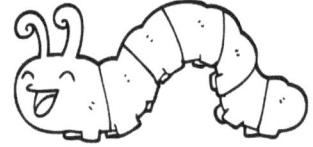

Clawdia who?

Clawdia way through the internet to find this joke, let me in for a live performance!

Knock Knock.

Purrsonal

Who's there?

Purrsonal who?

Purrsonal trainer here to get you and your cat in shape! Ready for some paw-lates?

Knock Knock.

Kitten

Who's there?

Kitten who?

Kitten around, can't you tell? Let me in for some real fun!

Knock Knock.

Who's there?

Meowtivate

Meowtivate who?

Meowtivate you to open this door, I've got some purr-sonal jokes to share!

Knock Knock.

Who's there?

Catticus

Catticus who?

Catticus Finch, ready to defend the right to nap in sunny spots all day!

Knock Knock.

Mew

Who's there?

Mew who?

Mew-ser, I've been waiting to serenade you with my midnight song

Knock Knock.

Furry

Who's there?

Furry who?

Furry-ous about the lack of treats, open up, and let's negotiate!

Clever cats craftily catch cautious critters.

How many clever cats can craftily catch cautious critters if clever cats could catch critters craftily?

Frisky felines flip finely for fanciful feathers.

How many frisky felines must flip finely to fetch fanciful feathers if frisky felines found feathers fanciful?

Purring Persians prance past plush purple pillows.

How many purring Persians can prance past plush purple pillows if purring Persians prefer prancing past pillows plushly purple?

Six sly Siamese silently sneak by six sleek sofas.

How many sly Siamese can silently sneak if six sleek sofas stand by silently?

Quirky kittens quickly quiz on quirky quantum queries.

How quickly can quirky kittens quiz if quirky quantum queries quench their curiosity?

Fluffy felines fancifully flicking fluffy feathers furiously.

How furiously can fluffy felines flick if fanciful fluffy feathers fly by furiously?

Chatty calicos crafting clever cardboard condos.

How many chatty calicos can craft if clever cardboard condos call for crafting?

Bouncy Bengals balancing on bright blue balls.

How many bouncy Bengals can balance if bright blue balls beckon Bengals to bounce?

Mischevious Maine Coons mastering mysterious maze maneuvers.

How many mischievous Maine Coons can master if mysterious mazes mandate mastering maneuvers?

Plucky Persian kittens playfully pouncing on pink puffy pillows.

How many plucky Persian kittens can playfully pounce if pink puffy pillows are plentiful?

Daringly dexterous tabby cats dodge dozens of dangling toys daily.

How many daringly dexterous tabby cats does it take to dodge dozens of dangling toys daily?

Sneaky Siamese siblings stealthily swipe savory salmon snacks.

How many sneaky Siamese siblings can stealthily swipe if savory salmon snacks are stashed securely?

Frantic felines fetching feathery fluff find funny frolics.

How many frantic felines fetching feathery fluff can find funny frolics in a flurry?

Curious cats concocting creamy catnip concoctions carefully.

How many curious cats can concoct if creamy catnip concoctions need to be concocted carefully?

Whiskered warriors whimsically whirl whisker-width wool balls.

How many whiskered warriors can whimsically whirl if whisker-width wool balls are what they whirl?

Clever kittens clambering over colorful, crinkly catnip cushions.

How many clever kittens can clamber if colorful, crinkly catnip cushions are crammed in corners?

Sassy Siamese spinning swiftly on slippery, shiny surfaces.

How swiftly can sassy Siamese spin if slippery, shiny surfaces are so splendid for spinning?

Purr-fectly poised Persians preen proudly, purring profoundly.

How many purr-fectly poised Persians can preen and purr if proudly purring Persians are profoundly preening?

Bold Bengals bounce by bushels of bouncy, bright balls.

How many bold Bengals can bounce if bushels of bouncy, bright balls beckon boldly?

Giggling ginger cats grasp glittery, gleaming gadgets gracefully.

How gracefully can giggling ginger cats grasp if glittery, gleaming gadgets are up for grabs?

Quizzical kittens quickly quibble over quirky quantum quarks.

How quickly can quizzical kittens quibble if quirky quantum quarks queue up for questioning?

Merry marmalade moggies make magnificent midnight meows.

How many merry marmalade moggies might make magnificent meows at midnight if marmalade moggies meow magnificently?

Twisty tabbies take tiny, tippy-toe trips to tantalizing toy towns.

How many twisty tabbies can take tiny trips if tippy-toe trips to tantalizing toy towns are taken tonight?

Furry felines finagle fish from fanciful, frosty fridges.

How many furry felines can finagle fish if fanciful, frosty fridges are filled with fishy feasts?

Picky Persian princes prance past plush purple pillows, purring proudly.

How many picky Persian princes can prance and purr if plush purple pillows are placed precisely past their paths?

Crafty calico cats concoct curious catnip cocktails, causing chaos.

How many crafty calico cats can concoct if curious catnip cocktails consistently cause chaotic capers?

Sleek Siamese sailors sail seven salty seas, seeking sun-soaked shores.

How many sleek Siamese sailors can sail if seven salty seas are sought for sun-soaked shores to snooze and sunbathe?

Fluffy felines frolic freely, flaunting fanciful feathered toys.

How many fluffy felines can frolic and flaunt if fanciful feathered toys are flung freely?

Dapper dancing domestic cats dazzle during the dramatic dusk.

How many dapper dancing domestic cats can dazzle if dramatic dusk descends during their delightful dance?

Quirky quartets of quivering kittens quietly query quizzical quests.

How many quirky quartets of quivering kittens can quietly query if quizzical quests quench their curious quests?

Brave Bengal brothers balance boldly on bouncing, bubblegum balls.

How many brave Bengal brothers can balance if bouncing, bubblegum balls beckon boldly beneath blue skies?

Whimsical whiskered wizards weave wondrous, wispy, woolen webs.

How many whimsical whiskered wizards can weave if wondrous, wispy, woolen webs are what they wish to weave?

Sly, sleek, speckled sphynxes spy spicy, sizzling, savory snacks.

How many sly, sleek, speckled sphynxes can spy if spicy, sizzling, savory snacks are scattered so sparingly?

Cunning cats cunningly conceal countless colorful, chirping crickets.

How many cunning cats can cunningly conceal if countless colorful, chirping crickets chirp cunningly close?

Prancing patchwork pussycats parade past picturesque pumpkin patches.

How many prancing patchwork pussycats can parade if picturesque pumpkin patches provide the perfect path?

Tiptoeing tabby twins tackle towering tiers of teetering tuna tins.

How many tiptoeing tabby twins can tackle if towering tiers of teetering tuna tins tempt their tiny paws?

Six slinky Siamese silently slither, seeking savory sushi snacks.

How many slinky Siamese can silently slither if savory sushi snacks are secretly stashed for sneaky snacking?

Frantic furry felines flicker through the foggy, frosty, fern-filled forest.

How many frantic furry felines can flicker if a foggy, frosty, fern-filled forest forms the foreground for their frolic?

Mischievous Maine Coons mix magical, mystical melodies at midnight.

How many mischievous Maine Coons can mix if magical, mystical melodies are made at the moonlit midnight meeting?

Cheeky calicos chase chunky, chirpy chipmunks, causing cheerful chaos.

How many cheeky calicos can chase if chunky, chirpy chipmunks chomp cheerfully, causing chaotic chases?

Purring pixie bobcats play piano perfectly, producing peaceful, purring melodies.

How many purring pixie bobcats can play if pianos are perfectly poised for producing peaceful, purring melodies?

Boldly bounding Bengal babies bounce by bushy bushes, bewildering busy bees.

How many boldly bounding Bengal babies can bounce if bushy bushes brim with bewildering, busy bees buzzing by?

Vivacious velvet Vikings venture valiantly with varied, vibrant violets and very vocal vanishing vixen cats.

How many vivacious velvet Vikings can venture if varied, vibrant violets and very vocal vanishing vixen cats vie for their view?

Quirky quilled quokkas question quick-quipping, quiveringly quiet quilted quokkas in quaint, quirky quadrants.

How many quirky quilled quokkas can question if quick-quipping, quiveringly quiet, quilted quokkas quell queries in quaint, quirky quadrants?

Flickering fluorescent felines fancy frolicking fearlessly in fantastical, fluorescent, fairy-filled forests.

How many flickering fluorescent felines can fancy frolicking if fantastical, fluorescent, fairy-filled forests foster their fearless flights?

I'm not a lion, but I can be found in a pride; I'm not a house, but I can have many rooms.

What am I?

Answer: A cat mansion

I can jump higher than a house, run faster than a car, but I dread water like a witch

What am I?

Answer: A scaredy-cat with a vivid imagination.

I'm known to walk silently, but my presence is always known. I can disappear into the night, yet my eyes give away my throne

What am I?

Answer: A cat on a moonlit prowl

I have nine lives but no soul, I can climb a tree but can't reach a goal. I might chase a mouse or a laser light, but in a box, I'll spend the night

What am I?

Answer: A domestic house cat with ambitious dreams and a cardboard box

I nap in a sunbeam and vanish at dinnertime, only to appear when you open a can

What am I?

Answer: A cat with an internal can opener alarm

I have whiskers but don't shave, and I'll chase a dot but not catch it

What am I?

Answer: A laser-pointer-obsessed cat

I'm the king of the jungle at home, but water turns me into a mouse

What am I?

Answer: A cat with a bath-time phobia

I climb higher than a tree but fear a tiny bee

What am I?

Answer: A brave-hearted house cat with a sensible fear of bees

I can leap tall fences in a single bound but vanish at the sound of a vacuum

What am I?

Answer: A superhero cat with a kryptonite vacuum

I wear a fur coat year-round but never get hot. I love climbing trees but hate getting wet

What am I?

Answer: A cat with a natural aversion to baths and an affinity for tree adventures

I have ears that can hear a pin drop, but I ignore you when you call my name

What am I?

Answer: A selectively deaf cat

I'm an expert at hide and seek, often found in places you never seek

What am I?

Answer: A cat in its latest secret sleeping spot

I guard the house with silent meows, but I'm not a dog. I can leap five times my height, but I'm not a frog

What am I?

Answer: A cat with ambitions of grandeur

I can disappear into a box smaller than me, and emerge as if from a magician's hat

What am I?

Answer: A cat, the master of fitting into impossible spaces

I'm the best at catching shadows, yet I never win a race

What am I?

Answer: A cat chasing the elusive light beam

I can make a bed out of anything, but I choose the box over a king-sized bed

What am I?

Answer: A cat, the ultimate minimalist

I have a tail that I chase, but I'm not chasing my own story

What am I?

Answer: A cat mesmerized by its tail

I speak without words, often in the dead of night, demanding an audience

What am I?

Answer: A cat with a midnight song to share

I'm a skilled acrobat who never joined the circus, and my favorite act is the midnight zoom

What am I?

Answer: A cat performing the nightly zoomies

I can turn a simple box into a castle, but I've never studied architecture

What am I?

Answer: A cat, the imaginative interior designer

I can see in the dark but stumble in daylight over air

What am I?

Answer: A cat, the night-time ninja with a daylight dilemma

I demand the finest seat in the house, but I never bought a ticket

What am I?

Answer: A cat, the entitled audience of one

I have a throne that often moves, yet I remain the king

What am I?

Answer: A cat atop a roomba

I'm known to walk on keyboards, but not to type. Instead, I leave messages of a different kind

What am I?

Answer: A cat, the unintentional typist

I'm a master of stealth by day and a vocal performer by night

What am I?

Answer: A cat, the day sleeper and night serenader

I can vanish into thin air only to reappear when least expected

What am I?

Answer: A cat, the master of surprise entrances and exits

I may look like I'm plotting the world's takeover at one moment and chasing my own shadow the next

What am I?

Answer: A cat with grand ambitions and simple pleasures

I'm known for my curiosity, but it's never killed me... yet

What am I?

Answer: A cat on its ninth life, living dangerously

I'm the ruler of a kingdom that's often soft and cozy, yet I prefer a cardboard box

What am I?

Answer: A cat, the sovereign of snug spaces

I can leap tall shelves in a single bound and knock items down without a sound

What am I?

Answer: A cat, the silent sentinel of the night

I have a built-in alarm for meals but no concept of time

What am I?

Answer: A cat, the punctual yet timeless diner

I often sit like a loaf, but I'm not made of bread

What am I?

Answer: A cat, perfecting the art of the loaf pose

www.ingramcontent.com/pod-product-compliance
Lightning Source LLC
Chambersburg PA
CBHW071035080526
44587CB00015B/2625